Wildflowers

Eshwardai Ramsaywack

BookLeaf Publishing

Presentation by *BookLeaf Publishing*

Web: www.bookleafpub.com

E-mail: info@bookleafpub.com

ISBN: 9789357445641

First edition 2022

DEDICATION

This book is dedicated to everyone that suffers with insecurities or feels that they don't belong. Especially to those that compare themselves to others and live their lives in the shadow of someone else. It is time you embrace your flaws and love yourself. Because you are capable of more than you can imagine. You are a work in progress and you will get to where you want to be. But it takes time. Trust the process.

ACKNOWLEDGEMENT

To my wonderful readers. Thank you for your love and support. This one's for you .

Be You

Be you. Be your true self.
Be silly and weird, and wear your soul so
everyone can see.
Express your emotions without a care of what
others may perceive you to be.
Love everything about you, don't wait for others
to love you first.
Bask within your glowing radiance.

Imperfect

I know I'm not perfect, for my flaws define me.
from a child to a grown adult, I've been seeking
validation, trying to be a better me.
I can change my appearance if that's what's
desired. For a few nip and tuck work hurt as
much, for the price of acceptance.
As my hunger for approval takes me beyond my
limit.
I know I'm not perfect. But am I beautiful now?

Love ❤

Love, love as hard as you can.
Love with everything you've got.
Love like there's no tomorrow.
Love the way you want to be loved.
But never lose yourself as you love.
Because if you lose yourself as you love, you'll
never love again. Because to truly love, you
must first love yourself.

LightHouse

My brightness is not the light you desire.
I'm merely invisible, to not only you but the
world.
And everything I do is not seen.
But tomorrow I'll shine so bright, it'll be a light
you've never seen before.
A light unseen by all, near and far, and time
would've been my greatest achievement.
As you'll live with the regret of not allowing
me to shine when my light was faint, for all I
needed was to be recognized.
And now with time, I'm seen from a distance.

Finding Me

I've avoided traveling the road that leads to finding me. As I've become scared to see what my road leads to, so I seek comfort in traveling yours with you. As I watch you grow and glow while I remain small, as my light fades away. I saw it was time to start my own journey.

I Am Happiness

I was searching for happiness.
I lifted and tossed every moving and breathing
being in hope to find it.
I seek validation from those who knew not what
happiness is and their bitter half love they gave
to me, I accepted it because it made me feel.
I was on the urge to find happiness but along the
way I lost myself more, because I seek it in all
the wrong places and all the wrong people.
Happiness was in front of me, but I refused to
see it. I refuse to acknowledge it. I didn't
think finding happiness would've been so easy. I
believed I needed to give my all in order to find
happiness. In order to be happy. But I was
wrong.
I came to realize, happiness starts with me, for
I'm responsible for my own happiness.
I am happiness.

I Am Happiness

You Are Worthy Of It All

Only you can and will always be there for you. Sometimes you have to be strong, even when it seems as if the world is against you. You have to believe that you can and you will overcome all battles. Because only you can fight for you. You have to know that you are worth fighting for. You have to come to terms and realize that you are enough and have always been and will forever be.

 You have overcome many obstacles and have survived far too much to give up now, to stop fighting. You need to remind yourself like It's a daily mantra.
"You are worthy"
"You are loved"
"You are wanted"
"You are strong and capable and can conquer it all"

You are uniquely spectacular and nothing or no one can stop you from achieving your dreams and desires.
Yes! Many will hate you because you're growing and glowing and have chosen you over them. But it's time you did that. It is time you choose yourself.

You need to know that you deserve the love that you're giving everyone else.
You deserve it all! You need to keep fighting and be strong for yourself.
Because you are capable of more than you can imagine. You are worthy of it all!

Broken

I knew you were broken.
But I thought that I could mend you. I thought
that I could take you under my wings and love
you as you slowly become whole again.
But little did I know; your intentions were never
to be amended.
But to break me beyond fixing.
Little did I know, you gained happiness from
watching me suffer.
For I should have known that there's only
loneliness and darkness for a broken soul.

Searching For The Light

I truly hope that one day,
you'll understand that I had to leave.
I gave you my every light,
and when I became dark,
we lost sight of each other, our souls were dark
alike.
I needed to see where I was going.
With you, I could no longer tell.
Now here I am, searching for the light in
someone else.

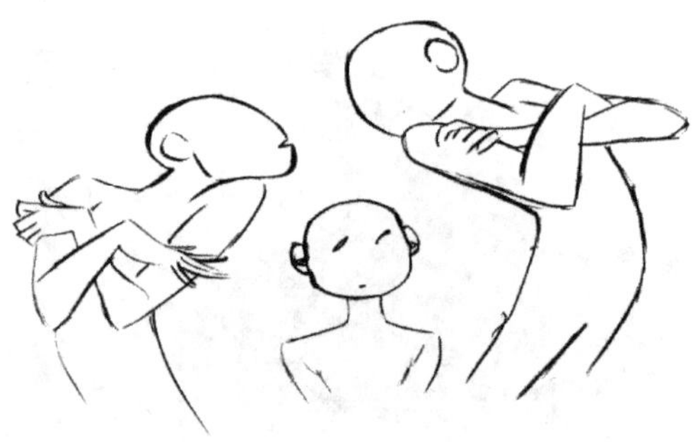

Maybe

It's not that I'm difficult to love.
It's just, no one has ever loved me.
It's not that I'm bitter and composed of only
darkness.
It's just, I don't know how to express my
emotions.

I think I'm becoming invisible. Everyone denies
me and no one truly loves me.
Maybe they can see the person I truly am.
The person I'm unable to see.
Maybe they've tried to love me, but I'm
unlovable.

Maybe, it's just me.

?.

Sometimes, when I'm alone, my mind takes me
to places beyond.
As I reflect on my past, present and future.
I wonder if I'll ever find anyone that would
really and truly understands me.

Loving Yourself

We are often told that we can never truly love
without learning to love ourselves first .

But no one has ever told us that loving ourselves
is not as easy as saying it.

Loving ourselves is an art that cannot be taught.
But an art that we ourselves gain as we learn to
accept our every flaw.
It's an art that takes years to master and a few
seconds to forget.

But , always remember that in order to master
any art of life, we will fail a thousand times.
So continue trying to master the art of loving
yourself. Even if you fail along the way, keep
trying and remember that from our failures
comes strength.

Why Can't You Be Happy?

Why can't you be happy?
Look into the mirror and tell me what you see.

The reflection in your eyes tells me you can only
see your flaws.
You point them out as if it's a contest and you
must win them all.

I see the way you look at yourself , as you hate
every inch of your body each day.

I see you as you grab your thighs and you poison
your mind with disgust about yourself.

I can hear you telling yourself that skinny jeans
are your worst nightmare . As your thighs will
have them bursting at the seam.

I can hear you aloud. You can't see me, but I can
see you.

Why can't you be happy?

Look into the mirror and tell me what you see.

Tugging at your skin and pulling at your belly in
hope that you'll see another rib appear.

Disappointed you become, because you're the
same as yesterday.

You questioned yourself,
What's happening?
You've avoided food as much as you can, and
the little that you ate, came back out with the
force of your hand.

Why can't you be happy?
Look into the mirror and tell me what you see.

I hear you aloud, thinking to yourself;
Should I skip dessert,
Should I put the muffin down?
All the other girls are done, but here I am for
another round.

Disappointed you become.
Because you're the same as yesterday.
You've become horrified by your sight.

You tell yourself nothing looks good. You can't
wear a crop top because you fear everyone will
stare.

Why can't you be happy?
Look into the mirror and tell me what you see.
As you stand and stare at the reflection of
yourself, calculating the many pounds you've
lost and how close you are to your goal.

You're becoming weary and tired , lifeless and
sick. But that does not worry you. From 100-15
you have never felt so alive.

Why can't you be happy?
Look into the mirror and tell me what you see.

I can hear you aloud, you can't see me, but I can
see you.

Look into the mirror I am you.

Why can't you accept yourself?
Happiness does not come from being a
particular size.
Look into the mirror, it's right in front of you,
Look into the mirror,
thick or thin
Heavy or light

Happiness is right there inside you.

Pain & Hurt

Do you know what really hurts ?
Laying in bed at night , and it's so quiet.
Frightening quiet , not even the wind makes a
sound . And loneliness takes over your entire
being, as your body becomes numb to the pain
you're feeling. But yet at the same time it hurts
so much, and all you can do is cry and scream .
But even then , there's no noise. Your scream is
silent from the pain and hurt .

Imagination

Let your imagination roam free like wildflowers that can't be controlled.

Live Life On Your Own Path.

You are going to meet many people in your lifetime. Some will adore you while others won't . And that's ok . You can't control how others receive your energy . But do know , that you can't control your life based on others opinions of you.
Live life on your own path.

Give Yourself Permission

Give yourself permission to be happy. Yesterday came and went , and it may not have been as amazing as you'd wish . But , today is a new day , filled with endless possibilities. Today you can start fresh ! Focus on the things you need , and make peace with what you can't have.

Like The Ocean

I'm like the waves of the ocean.
Thunderous and clam .

The Torch Is In Your Hand

I believe we've all seen better days .
But, we've also seen worse.
But that doesn't mean we must dwell on the bad
and allow negative thoughts to keep us down .
We have to stop blaming ourselves for
opportunities missed. Quit focusing on what we
didn't do when we had the chance and start
focusing on what we can do and how we can
better ourselves each day. Because dwelling on
yesterday can cause no good for our tomorrows.
You have the power for change.
The torch is in your hand.

The torch is in your hand.

The Choice Is Yours

In a world where you have the choice to be kind
and beautiful, why do you choose to be ugly?

Instead of spreading your love like clear running
water that reaches every heart and quenches the
thirst of weary souls, you make the choice to
spread your hate like a deadly virus.

You have the choice to make a difference.
A positive one.

But yet you choose not to. You chose to fuel the
hate and become bitter as ever. know it's not too
late to change your ways.

You have free-will to choose right from wrong.
Choose wisely and make a change that benefits
all. A change to stand together and unite as one.
The choice is yours.

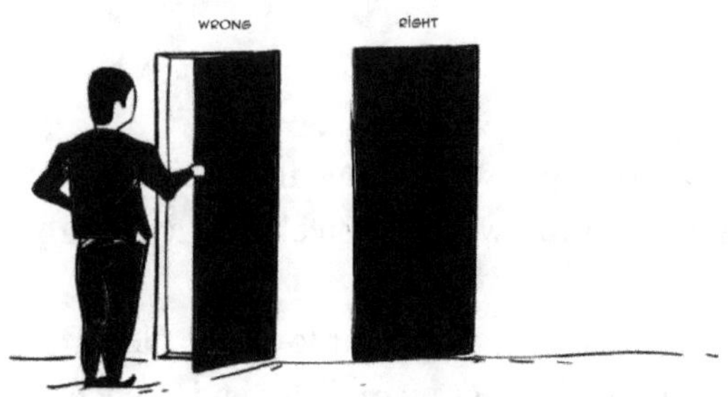

WRONG
RIGHT

You Are Amazing

You are so much more than the opinions of others . So don't allow the negative words of others to bring you down. Their negativity does not define you as a person , you are beyond what they think of you.
You are amazing !!

www.ingramcontent.com/pod-product-compliance
Lightning Source LLC
LaVergne TN
LVHW051246200726

843510LV00011B/1704